Cracks in the Sidewalk

Cracks in the Sidewalk

Crystal Bowman

Illustrations by Joel E. S. Tanis

2D EDITION

Baker Books

A Division of Baker Book House Co
Grand Rapids, Michigan 49516

Published by Baker Books
a division of Baker Book House Company
P.O. Box 6287, Grand Rapids, MI 49516-6287

Printed in the United States of America

Library of Congress Cataloging-in-Publication Data

Bowman, Crystal.
    Cracks in the sidewalk / Crystal Bowman ; illustrated by Joel Tanis.
        p.   cm.
    Summary: A collection of poems capturing the trials and adventures in a child's life.
    ISBN 0-8010-1227-9 (cloth)
    1. Children's poetry, American [1. American poetry.]
  I. Tanis, Joel E., ill. II. Title
  PS3551.O87563 C7 2001
  811'.54—dc21   2001035989

For current information about all releases from Baker Book House, visit our web site:

http://www.bakerbooks.com

To

Bob,
Rob,
Scott,
and Teri,
with love

Special thanks to
Frank J. Hackinson
Nancy Faber
Randall Faber

Come with Me

Come with me and you will see
A world of sweet reality,
Where happiness and love are free,
And things are how they ought to be.
Sometimes tranquil, sometimes wild,
'Tis the world of an innocent child.

Contents

School Days

An Apple a Day

In the Kitchen

Daily Adventures

In My Room

Little People

hee
hee
hee

Why?

Why do cows make milk?
Why do bees make honey?
Why does rain fall from the sky?
Why are summers sunny?

Why do mice eat cheese?
Why do babies cry?
Why are zebras black and white?
Why do robins fly?

Why do cats have kittens?
Why do hens lay eggs?
Why do stars come out at night?
Why do flies have legs?

I have so many questions
And often wonder, why?
I have a lot of things to learn;
I'm just a little guy.

No Such Thing

There's no such thing as monsters,
The sandman's make-believe.
Leprechauns are just a myth,
Intended to deceive.

Witches, ghosts, and goblins
Don't scare me anymore.
Fairies, elves, and unicorns
Are actually a bore.

I'm old enough to know that
These things are just pretend.
But please don't say a word to my
Imaginary friend.

Sit Still

My father says to sit up straight,
My mother says, "Don't squirm!"
They say that I remind them
Of a wiggle, wiggle worm.
My ankles get so tired
When they're hanging in the air.
They feel a whole lot better
When I rest them on my chair.
Sitting still in grown-up chairs
Is really quite a chore.
But life will be more pleasant
When my feet can touch the floor.

Success

I finally did it,
I'm so very proud!
I finally did it,
I'll shout it out loud!

Couldn't do it before
Though I tried and I tried.
And now I can do it,
I'm bursting with pride.

Let me tell you about
My very good news:
Today I learned how
To tie my own shoes!

Magic Wand

I have a pretty magic wand
With glitter on the end.
I've learned to use it wisely,
It's almost like a friend.
When my room is messy
And cleaning is a chore,
I wave my magic wand
And touch the toys upon the floor.
Then suddenly they come alive
And much to my surprise,
They quickly put themselves away
Before my very eyes.
Another trick I like to do
Is when it's time to eat,
I wave my wand across the food
So everything tastes sweet.

I turn my soup to ice cream
And eat it right away.
These magic tricks are wonderful!
I do them every day.
If you don't have a magic wand
Just find yourself a stick.
Use your imagination
And do a magic trick!

Sometimes

Sometimes I'm an astronaut
Exploring outer space.
Sometimes I'm a circus clown
And wear a silly face.

Sometimes I'm a dancer;
I dance all around the floor.
Sometimes when I stomp and romp,
I pretend I'm a dinosaur.

Sometimes I drive a freight train,
'Cause I'm the engineer.
Sometimes I'm a magician
And make things disappear.

Sometimes I just buzz around
Like a big ol' bumblebee.
And when I'm done pretending
I go back to being me.

A Picture for Mama

"Mama, I drew a nice picture for you,
Right there on the wall,
And I painted it too!
I drew all those flowers
And painted them green.
Isn't it truly a wonderful scene?
I made one for you,
And I made one for me.
These pictures are beautiful;
Don't you agree?"
My mother just stood there
With tears in her eyes.
I could tell by her face
That she loved my surprise!

Someone Else's Birthday

It's someone else's birthday;
That's the way it always is.
The birthday party's never mine,
It's always hers or his.

> I do like going to parties
> And playing birthday games.
> But the letters on the birthday cake
> Spell someone else's name.

My friend is so excited;
His birthday's almost here.
But I won't have a birthday
For at least another year.

That's why I'm so unhappy
And feeling sad today.
You see, I had my birthday
Only yesterday.

I Wish I Could Whistle!

I sure wish that I could whistle!
I practice every day.
Everyone else can do it,
At least it seems that way.

Every time I try it,
I hold my lips just so.
I fill my mouth with lots of air,
And then I blow and blow.

But no, I never whistle,
I only blow lots of air.
Perhaps someday I will do it,
By then, I probably won't care.

Little Sister

I have a little sister
With curly golden hair.
I like to read her stories
And rock her in the chair.

She's so much fun to play with.
She's small and cute and funny.
She loves her teddy bear
And her furry, yellow bunny.

I love my little sister.
I'm proud to be her brother.
But when she has a dirty pants
I bring her to my mother.

Sidewalks

Sidewalks are for hopscotch
Or taking an afternoon stroll.
Sidewalks are for riding bikes
Or watching marbles roll.

Sidewalks take you to your friends
Where you can run and play.
Sidewalks are for splashing
When it's a rainy day.

Sidewalks are for roller skates
Or drawing pictures with chalk.
Sidewalks are for picnics
Where kids can sit and talk.

Sidewalks are a happy place
Where little ones can roam.
And when it's time for dinner,
They always take you home.

Man in the Moon

Have you ever seen the man in the moon?
I've seen his eyes and nose.

But where in the world are his arms and legs,
And where are his fingers and toes?

I'm really not sure there's a man in the moon,
'Cause all I've seen is his face.

Without a body it's not a man—
It's just a head in space!

Friends and
Neighbors

Alan

Hello, my name is Alan,
And I would like to say,
I spell my name A-L-A-N
And that's the only way!

Some folks put in extra L's;
Some spell it with an E.
When people spell my name all wrong,
It really bothers me!

So if you want to be my friend,
I'll tell you one more time:
Please spell my name correctly
And things will be just fine.

My Neighbor Ned

My neighbor Ned has hairy toes;
It seems the hair just grows and grows.
He combs it and curls it
And styles with mousse.
I told him to cut it,
But it was no use.

He dyes it yellow, red, and blue.
He spikes it and rats it
And frizzes it too.
He twists it in braids
And ties it with bows.
He washes his hair
With the garden hose.

He dries it with dryers
And sprays it with spray.
He cares for his hair
Many hours each day.
He's rather strange,
My neighbor Ned,
With hair on his toes
Instead of his head.

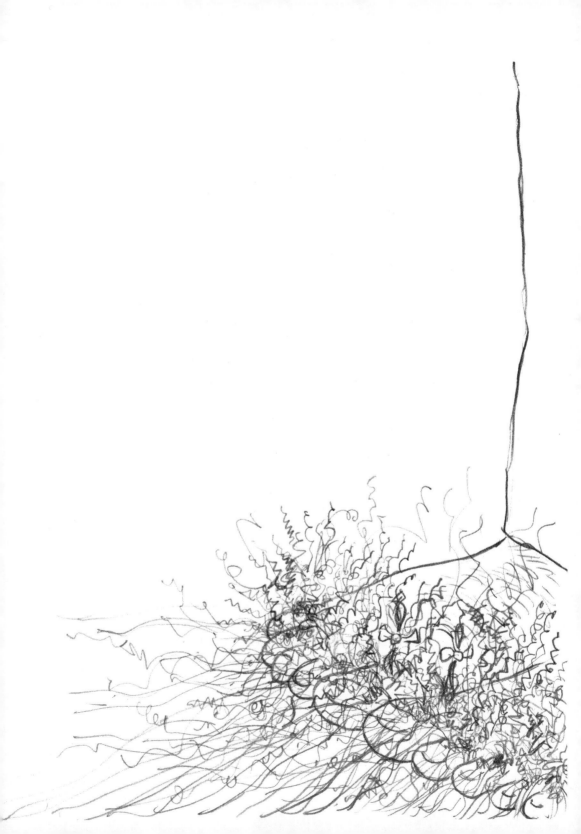

Messy Bess

I had a friend named messy Bess,
Whose bedroom always was a mess.
She never ever made her bed,
Nor put away the books she read.
She never put her clothes away,
But left them on the floor to stay.

Her toys were scattered everywhere,
And dolls were piled on her chair.
Her mom and dad did all they could
To make her change; it did no good.
She always kept her room a mess.
That's why we called her messy Bess.

But then the circus came to town,
With acrobats and a silly clown.
Her family went to see the show,
But messy Bess, she could not go.
She couldn't find her coat or shoes,
Or the money she had planned to use.
When everybody said good-bye,
Messy Bess began to cry.

She learned a lesson on that day
And put her clothes and shoes away.
She cleaned her room and made her bed
And put away the books she read.
Well, since that day her room's been clean,
So now we call her clean Marlene.

Charles

Charles had snarls all over his hair.
His hair was too long, and he just didn't care.
He never took time for a brush or a comb;
His hair looked so bad that he had to stay home.
For when he went out, all the people would stare
At Charles with snarls all over his hair.

Then one day he went to a barbershop,
And he said to the barber, "These snarls must stop!"
The barber took scissors, a razor, and cream,
And he cut and he shaved 'til his head was all clean.
Then Charles got up, and he walked out the door,
While his snarls lay still on the barbershop floor.

Now when he goes out the people still stare.
Charles' snarls are gone, and so is his hair.

Marilyn May and Mike

I know a girl named Marilyn May
Who has a brother named Mike.
The problem is, that Marilyn May
And her brother look almost alike.
They get so upset if you get their names wrong,
And you can't tell the one from the other.
But I never quite know if it's Marilyn May
Or if it's maybe her brother.
Each time I see them I'm very confused,
And I really don't know what to say.
So instead of getting them very upset,
I usually just walk away.
Well, I've finally found a solution
For these siblings who look just alike.
From now on, if I should meet one of them,
I'll just call it Marilyn Mike.

Walter

Why did they name me Walter?
I wish it were Peter or Paul.
I wish it were Scott or Samuel;
Walter's the worst name of all.

It could have been Bobby or Billy,
Or Johnny, Jason, or Jim.
It could have been Ryan or Robby,
Or Tommy, Terry, or Tim.

Oh, why did they name me Walter?
I'd like to be Danny or Don.
I'd like to be Michael or Marcus,
Or Reggie, Randy, or Ron.

Oh, why did they name me Walter?
It's the very worst name in the world.
I hate to complain at the sound of a name,
But, you see, it's because I'm a girl.

Friends

A friend is someone who listens,
A friend is someone who cares.
A friend is someone who understands,
A friend is someone who shares.

It's nice to have a special friend
To tell all your secrets to.
It's nice to know that someone you like
Is someone who really likes you.

A friend is someone you call on the phone
To talk about nothing at all.
A friend is someone who cheers you up
And makes you feel ten feet tall.

Everyone would like to have
A special friend, it's true.
But if you want a special friend,
You need to be one too.

Sarah Kissed Me

Sarah kissed me on the cheek;
My stomach felt a little weak.
My heart was pounding in my ear—
That's how it is when Sarah's near.

We shared some taffy, soft and chewy;
Her kiss was sticky, wet, and gooey.
I think I'll leave it there a week—
'Cause Sarah kissed me on the cheek.

Peculiar Pete

Peculiar Pete has two left feet,
And both his hands are right.
He goes to bed with the morning sun
And stays awake all night.

He washes his hair with applesauce
And bathes in oyster stew.
He brushes his teeth with tomato paste
And gargles with shampoo.

He wears his clothing backwards;
He uses his nose to eat.
And that is why my friends and I
Call him peculiar Pete.

Where Are My Friends?

I'm walking up and down the street
Hoping that by chance I'll meet
Someone who will want to play
On this warm and sunny day.

It seems that no one is around,
One single friend cannot be found.
I guess I'll have to go back home,
Where I will sit and be alone.
But as I reach my house I see
My friends have come to play with me!

Gathered at my own front door
Are five or six or even more.
My friends have all come out to play
On this warm and sunny day.

46

Show and tell

School Days

School Days

On Monday, I wish I could watch TV,
But I have to go to school.

On Tuesday, I'd love to swim in the sea,
But I have to go to school.

On Wednesday, I'd like to ride my bike,
But I have to go to school.

On Thursday, I wish I could go for a hike,
But I have to go to school.

On Friday, I'd love to go to the zoo,
But I have to go to school.

On Saturday, there's not a thing to do,
I wish I could go to school.

My Lunch Box

When I come in from recess
I'm as hungry as a bear.
I open up my lunch box
And sit down in my chair.

First, I eat my cookie,
Then I eat my chips.
Then I use my napkin
To wipe my salty lips.

Next, I eat my apple;
My mother says I must.
I finally eat my sandwich,
But I never eat my crust.

Algebra

I've always liked arithmetic,
I think that it is great.
Two plus two adds up to four,
And four plus four is eight.

But now I'm learning algebra
And I am so perplexed!
Somehow three plus twenty-nine
Is Y or Z or X!

I don't like adding letters;
Letters are for words.
I'd rather work with numbers.
This math is for the birds!

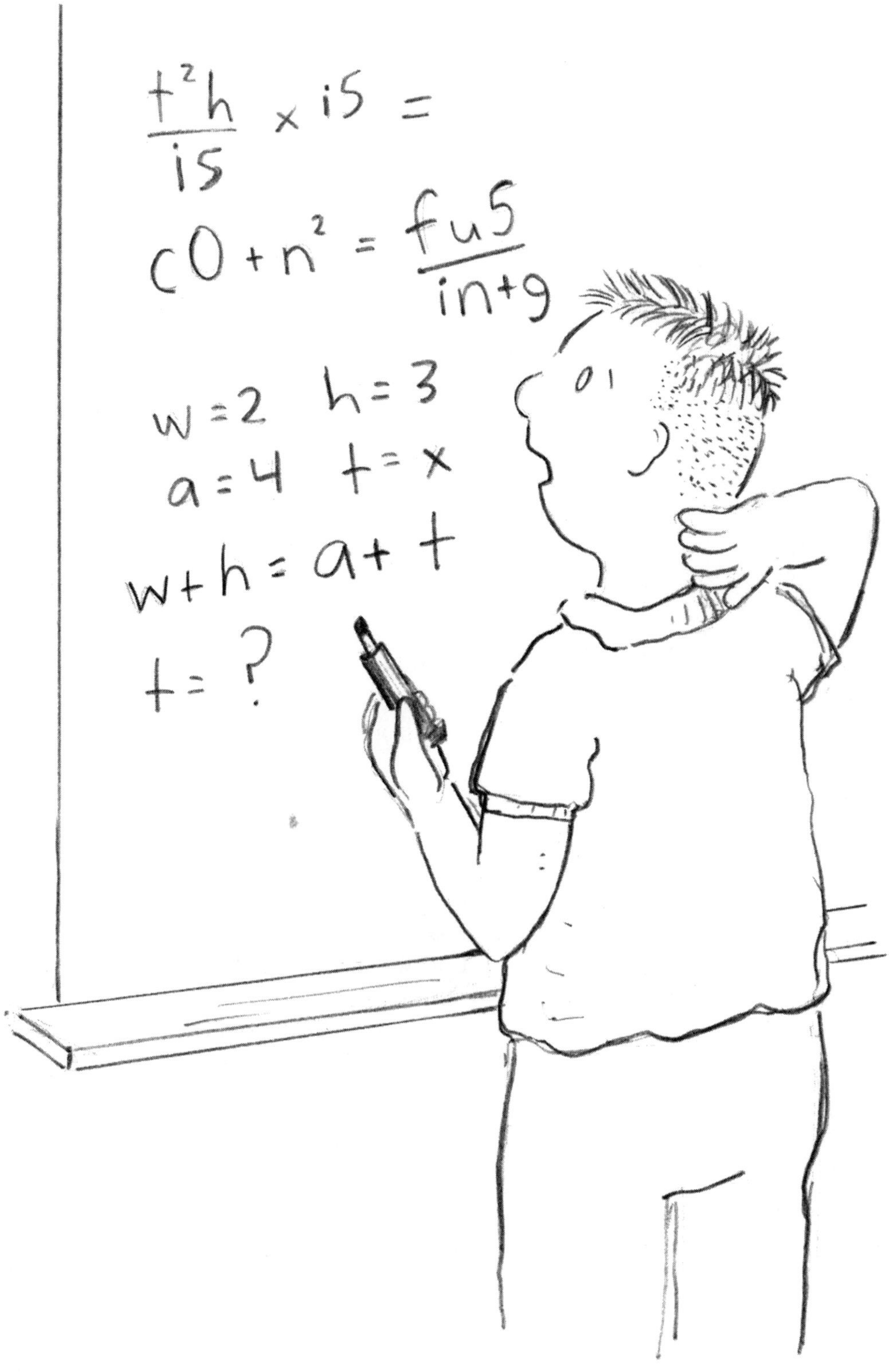
t²h / is × is =
c0 + n² = fu5 / in+9
w = 2 h = 3
a = 4 t = x
w + h = a + t
t = ?

Plurals

Plurals get me all mixed up,
Now let me tell you why—
One is called an octopus,
But two are octopi.
One little rodent is called a mouse,
And two or more are mice.
You shake and toss a single die,
But two of them are dice.

A long-neck bird is called a goose,
And two of them are geese.
But when you have an extra caboose,
You never say cabeese.
One utensil is called a knife,
But two of them are knives.
Trying to learn these plurals
Makes me break out in hives.

A buck or doe is called a deer,
But two are also deer.
I'll never learn these plurals
If I study them all year.
The plural of fish is fishes,
But sometimes it has to be fish.
These rules are so confusing,
I have one single wish:
To change a word to plural,
You simply add an "s."
But that is not the rule,
And so I have to guess!

The Play

I have a very important part
In the fifth-grade Christmas play.
I've practiced and I've memorized
The words I'm going to say.

I have the most important part;
I've got to get it right.
Perhaps I'll be a famous star
On center stage tonight.

I'm just a little nervous;
In fact, I'm really scared!
That's why I've practiced and rehearsed;
I need to be prepared.

I think I'll practice one more time;
Let's see, it goes like this:
"Thanks for coming here tonight;
Now you are dismissed."

Tuna Sandwich

I got my brother's sandwich
In my lunch box by mistake.
This one smells like tuna fish;
It's not the kind I take.
I cleared my throat politely,
I raised my hand and said,
"Would anybody like to trade
For tuna fish on bread?"

Freddie took my sandwich
And gave me chocolate cake.
Maybe there are just a few more
Trades that I can make.
"Would anybody like to have
This piece of colby cheese?"
Katie said, "I'll eat it!"
So I said, "Take it, please!"

She gave me her potato chips
And oatmeal cookie too.
Perhaps I'll make another trade
Before this lunch is through.
I gave away my cookie
For a brownie and some gum.
I never knew that eating lunch
At school could be such fun.

My lunch was so delicious;
I savored every bite.
The brownie and the cookie
Were truly a delight!
I ate all my potato chips
And Freddie's chocolate cake.
My brother's tuna sandwich
Was a wonderful mistake!

My Paper Monster

Oh, his legs look like spaghetti,
And his nose is round and green.
He has got the most enormous eyes
That you have ever seen.
He is ugly, he is scary,
That is why I love him so.
He's my very own creation,
And I'm proud to tell you so.

He's my awesome paper monster
That I made at school today.
And he's going to be so helpful
'Cause he'll chase the girls away.
I'll put him by my bedroom door
To keep my sister out.
As soon as she encounters him,
I know she'll scream and shout.

Oh, I know he'll cause excitement
Like I've never seen before.
He is such a great creation,
I think I'll make some more!

keep out
NO gerls
allOwd
(NO sisters
eether)

Wormy Day

It rained last night,
The earth is damp,
There's moisture in the air.
And as I walk to school today,
Worms are everywhere.

Long worms, short worms,
Fat and thin,
Squiggly, wiggly ones too.
I stop to count them, 1–2–3.
Number four crawls up my shoe.

I guess sometimes
The worms come out
To stretch and crawl around.
I guess when they get tired,
They'll wiggle back into the
ground.

Well, now it's time
To go to class,
So I'll be on my way.
It's interesting to walk to school,
When it's a wormy day.

Spelling Test

Why does pneumonia begin with a P?
It should begin with N.

Psychology should start with S;
I spelled it wrong again.

Knife should not begin with K,
Who spells it that way anyway?

And why does gnat begin with G?
It seems ridiculous to me!

I do not like these spelling words—
The craziest words I've ever heard!

This spelling test is not for me.
That's probably why I got a D.

An Apple a Day

Allergies

Get that cat
Away from me, please.
He's coming too close,
And he's making me sneeze.

Don't bring me flowers
When I'm sick in bed.
They stuff up my nose,
And they clog up my head.

When I eat peanuts,
Or candy, or cheese,
I break out in hives,
And I cough and I wheeze.

Wool makes me itch,
So I can't wear a sweater.
Without all my allergies,
Life would be better!

The Shot

I have to go and have a shot
For some disease I haven't got.
It makes no sense at all to me
To put myself through misery.

I'm healthy, strong, and feeling fine.
In two more weeks I'm turning nine.
I do not want to have a shot
For some disease I haven't got.

Vitamins

I must take my vitamins A, B, and C.
'Cause vitamins are very good for me.
A helps my ankles;
B strengthens my back.
C helps my collarbone, so it won't crack.
D feeds my brain, so I won't be dumb.
E gives me energy to help me run.
F makes me fast;
G makes me feel great.
H makes me happy; I hardly can wait!
By taking my vitamins, that's what I get.
So give me a dose of the whole alphabet.

Chicken Pox

Oh, look at all my horrid spots!
I think I've got the chicken pox.
They're on my arms and on my nose.
They're even in between my toes.
They're on my chest and in my hair,
These chicken pox are everywhere!
They're on my feet and elbows too.
I don't know what I'm going to do.
Twelve new spots appeared today.
I wish that they would go away,
So I could go outside to play.

Chocolate Medicine

Chocolate flavored medicine
Would taste so very good!
I know I'd gladly take it
If my mother said I should.
I would not make a face,
Or close my mouth, or turn my head.
I would not cause a fuss
Or go and hide beneath my bed.
If I had chocolate medicine,
I know I'd love the taste.
I'd finish every single drop;
It would not go to waste.
If I was ever feeling sick,
I'd take it right away.
And then I'd feel so good
That I would go outside to play.
Chocolate flavored medicine
Would never spoil or mold.
Will someone please invent it
Before I get too old?

Loose Tooth

My tooth came loose the other day.
It happened while I was at play.
I wiggled it with all my might,
Back and forth,
Left and right.

I twisted it around and 'round.
I pushed it up,
I pulled it down.
I couldn't take it anymore,
And so I tied it
To the door.

SLAM! BANG! Out it came.
A little blood,
A little pain.
And now I have a little hole;
It's where my tongue
Just seems to go.

The Singing Dentist

I really like my dentist
Except for just one thing.
Every time I visit him,
He always starts to sing.

A week ago last Monday—
And I'm telling you the truth,
He sang, "Don't Ever Leave Me,"
When he pulled my wisdom tooth.

If you have a favorite song,
Just ask him and he will,
Sing most any lyric
To the rhythm of his drill.

And if he doesn't know the words,
He'll just make up his own.
Sometimes he is so silly
That I roll my eyes and groan!

I really like my dentist,
And it wouldn't bother me
To hear his constant singing
If he learned to sing on key!

If You Don't

If you don't brush your teeth
They will surely fall out.

If you don't wash your face
You'll get pimples no doubt.

If you don't take a bath
You may get some disease.

If you don't blow your nose
You will probably sneeze.

If you don't clean your toes
They will maybe fall off.

If you don't wear your coat
You will get a bad cough.

If you don't drink your milk
You may never be strong.

So do all of this
And you'll never go wrong.

In the Kitchen

Cereal

Cereal is the very best food
That you could ever eat.
It's better than fruit or vegetables,
And it's certainly better than meat.

I wish I could eat it three times a day,
Every day of the year.
If I could be granted this simple request,
I'd dance on my tiptoes and cheer!

I love the kind with raisins and nuts
And the kind that has sugary flakes.
I like the way that it floats in my milk
And the sound that cereal makes.

Sometimes I eat it when no one's around—
I'm truly as sly as a fox.
But the kind I like best, above all the rest,
Is the kind with a prize in the box!

Peanut Butter Sandwich

In the pantry in our kitchen
There is food on every shelf.
There's a snack that I enjoy,
And I can get it by myself.

Whenever I'm feeling hungry,
And I need to fill my belly,
I find the peanut butter,
Get some bread and lots of jelly.

Then I make a tasty sandwich,
And I gobble every bite.
A peanut butter sandwich
Is a marvelous delight.

You can eat your cold bologna
Or enjoy some ham and cheese.
But for me, when I am hungry,
I say, "Peanut butter, please!"

Pizza Time

Pepperoni, sauce, and cheese,
May I have some pizza, please?
Chewy crusts are extra nice,
May I have another slice?

Who's that other pizza for?
May I have a little more?
Six more pieces, then I'll stop,
Wash it down with soda pop.

Feeling just a little stuffed,
I think that I have had enough.
Pepperoni, sauce, and cheese,
No more pizza for me, please!

Vegetables

Vegetables are the most horrible food,
I am really sorry to say!
My mother thinks I should eat some of them
Seven or eight times a day.

Spinach is soggy and smells like wet grass,
And I think that it comes from the sea.
Cabbage is fine for my mother and dad,
But it tastes awfully sour to me.

Beans can be yellow, or they can be green;
Broccoli looks like a tree.
Whatever the color or size or shape,
It certainly doesn't please me.

I do try to eat my vegetables,
But the ones I especially hate
I put on my fork and I hide every piece
Beneath the edge of my plate.

Don't blame me for not liking vegetables;
It really isn't my fault.
I'm sure whoever invented them
Must have been an adult.

Bug in My Stew

I was eating my stew,
Then decided to stop,
'Cause a bug was floating
Right there on the top.
I didn't get frightened
Or let out a shout;
I simply decided
To get the bug out.

The stew was delicious
I have to admit;
It tasted so good
That I ate quite a bit.
I finally finished,
And there in my mug,
Way at the bottom
I saw one more bug.

I could have been angry,
I could have been sad,
But the stew was the best
That I've ever had!
So when you are making
A flavorful stew,
Remember to throw in
A small bug or two.

Gingerbread Man

Once I made a gingerbread man.
I rolled him out and put him in a pan.
I put some candy on his face;
Oh, how delicious he will taste!
I put some raisins on his chest,
Buttons for his tiny vest.
I put him in the oven to bake;
What a yummy treat he'll make.

I took him out when he was done,
Eating him will be such fun!
I picked him up, I couldn't wait,
But then I put him on the plate.
He looked at me as if to say,
"Please, don't eat me up today!"
I smiled at him and shook my head.
I ate a candy bar instead.

Mother and Grandma

My mother feeds me tuna fish
With broccoli on the side.
But Grandma gives me candy
When my mouth is open wide.

My mother slices apples
And oranges for dessert.
My grandma brings me doughnuts
If she finds out I am hurt.

My mother makes me drink my milk
Most every single night.
But Grandma gives me ice cream bars
When I do something right.

My mother cooks up rice and beans
That have an awful taste.
So I say, "See ya later,
I'm going to Grandma's place!"

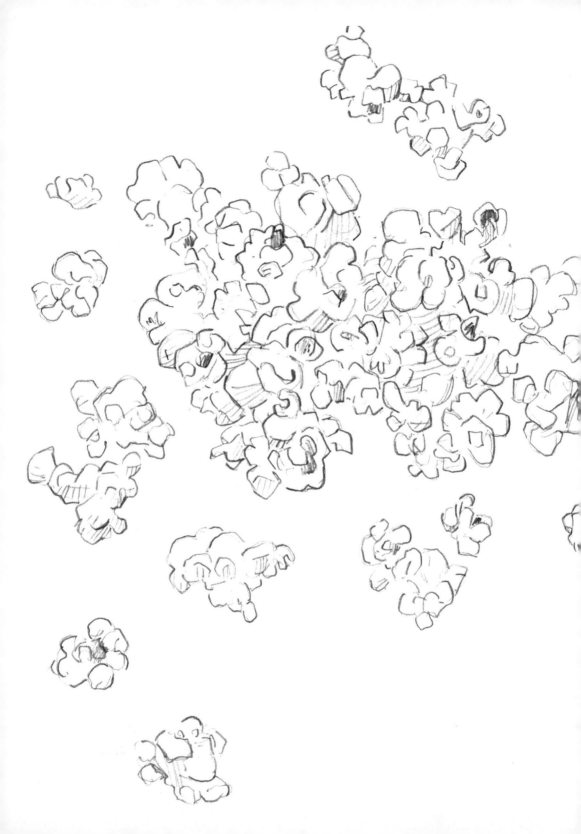

Popcorn

My brother makes popcorn every day,
That's all he ever eats.
He brings it with him everywhere
To share with people he meets.

Sometimes he eats it with butter and salt,
Sometimes he eats it plain.
Breakfast, lunch, and dinner too,
His meals are always the same.

This started several weeks ago,
We don't know how long it will last.
We're running out of popcorn
And my parents are aghast!

Since he's been eating popcorn,
It's weird to have him around.
He spends his days in unusual ways
Popping up and down.

The Alphabet

I came across the alphabet,
And this is what I found—
B and Z were backwards,
And Y was upside down.
K and N were inside out,
F was on its side.
Q and R were turned around,
And C was very wide.

M was fat, and L was thin;
A was chopped in half.
S and D were stuck together;
W made me laugh.
G was crooked; U was short.
P stood very tall.
I found the letters in my soup,
And so I ate them all!

I Roasted a Wiener

I roasted a wiener—
It tasted so good,
That I roasted and toasted
Everything I could.
I roasted a pickle,
A juicy tomato,
Some corn on the cob,
And a big, fat potato.

I roasted some mushrooms,
A thick T-bone steak,
A couple of perch,
And a cherry cheesecake.
Then I roasted a worm
And gave it a lick.
What yummy, delicious
Food on a stick!

93

Butterflies

There are butterflies
In my stomach;
I wish they would go away.
I wonder how they got there;
I wonder if they'll stay.

I feel them flying all around—
Flittering, fluttering upside down.
I'm dizzy and whizzy,
Not feeling so great.
Maybe it's from
Those caterpillars I ate.

The Spider

The spider spins his web so fine,
A geometric silk design.
A master plan, for therein lies,
A trap for unsuspecting flies.
He spins all day, then stops to rest,
Secure within his silky nest.

When he awakes, he's pleased to find
A tasty meal on which to dine.
Black flies, green flies, large and small.
The spider smiles and eats them all.
The moral, here, is short and sweet:
Those who work will also eat.

Baker's Blues

I tried to bake some cookies,
But I left them in too long.
I tried to bake a chocolate cake,
But everything went wrong!

I tried to make some brownies,
But I dropped them on the floor.
I think I'll stop this baking
And start heading for the store.

Daily Adventures

Cracks in the Sidewalk

My brother said be careful,
My sister said beware.
When you're walking on the sidewalk
You'd better walk with care.
You'd better pay attention
And listen to these facts,
'Cause your life will be in danger
If you step on any cracks.

You just might cause an earthquake
Or fall upon your nose.
When you're walking on the sidewalk
You'd better watch your toes.
And if you see a big one
That's long and deep and wide,
You'd better step on over
Or you'll tumble down inside.

And then you'll go to China,
Or maybe to Peru.
The cracks upon the sidewalk
Could be the end of you!
I listened to my sister
And I listened to my brother.
They really had me frightened,
So I went and told my mother.

Tree House

I built a nifty tree house
In a lovely maple tree.
I fell out of my tree house,
Broke my arm, and skinned my knee.

I built another tree house
From some lumber that I found.
My second nifty tree house
Is much closer to the ground.

Why Do I Laugh?

Why do I laugh, I do not know,
When my little sister stubs her toe?
Why do I howl and roll on the floor
When my mother walks into the bathroom door?

Why do I chuckle and cover my face
When my brother trips over his tennis shoelace?
Why do I giggle and hide in my bed
When my father stoops over and bumps his head?

Hey, wait a minute; stop laughing at me!
I fell off my chair and skinned my knee!

Mosquito Bite

Is there anyone out there
Who happens to know
How to get this mosquito bite
Off of my toe?

It itches and itches
And drives me berserk!
I've tried lots of remedies;
None of them work.

I wrapped it with tissue
And used special lotion.
My grandmother mixed up
Mosquito bite potion.

But still, it just itches
From morning till night.
My life's been disrupted
With this little bite!

Roller Skates

I found a pair of roller skates
And put them on my feet.
I thought I'd take a little ride
And skate across the street.

I thought I'd find a friend or two
Who'd like to skate along.
I thought I'd skate all afternoon,
But I was very wrong.

My feet went back and sideways,
My arms flew all around.
I wibbled and I wobbled
Till I landed on the ground.

I tried and tried a thousand times
Till I was black and blue.
So if you want some roller skates,
I have a pair for you!

My New Pet

I found him on the sidewalk;
He was cold and scared and wet.
I held him in my arms
And took him home to be my pet.

I washed him in the bathtub;
Things were going very well.
Then my mother came and asked me
Why she sensed a funny smell.

When she saw my little critter,
She fell down with a thunk.
Do you think that I should ask her
If she'll let me keep my skunk?

No Fair

My parents get to stay up late to watch a TV show,
But if I ask to join them, of course, they answer no!
They get to use the telephone most any time at all.
But I must ask permission before I make a call.

My father gets to have dessert before he eats his meat.
But I must finish all my food before I get a treat.
If Mother's room is messy, she simply shuts the door.
But I lose my allowance if my clothes are on the floor.

When Father belches loudly, he blames it on the food.
But if I make a little noise, they say I'm being rude.
My mother gets to use the car when she goes here or there,
But I must walk or use my bike; it really isn't fair!

My parents just came home from work; they've had a tiresome day.
While they prepare my dinner, I'm going outside to play.

The Tiny Bumblebee

I saw a tiny bumblebee
Just buzzin' through the air.
The bumblebee was not aware
That I was standing there.
So I began to chase him
Till he landed on a wall.
He looked so scared and helpless,
I was not afraid at all.
But then it seemed he noticed me
And followed me around.

I quickly tried to run away
But stumbled to the ground.
And then, that tiny bumblebee,
He did a nasty thing;
He sat upon my forehead
And gave me quite a sting!
This tragic little incident
Has made me very wise.
I've learned that I must never judge
Another by its size.

Forgetful Blues

I forgot to do my homework,
I forgot to tie my shoes.
I forgot to call my mother,
I forgot to pay my dues.
I forgot my lunch on Friday,
I forgot to do my chores.
I forgot to wear my jacket,
When I went to play outdoors.

I forgot to mail a letter,
I forgot to mow the lawn.
I forgot to say, "Excuse me,"
When I had a giant yawn.
I forgot to feed my goldfish,
I forgot to make my bed.
And now I know the problem,
I forgot to use my head.

Looking and Looking

Will somebody help me?
I'm losing my mind!
I'm looking for something
I simply can't find.

I know that I put it
Right over there.
And now I can't find it;
It's not anywhere.

I've looked by the window,
Behind every door,
I've looked in the closet
And searched every drawer.

It's not in the corners
Nor under the bed.
I'm truly convinced
That I'm losing my head.

Hey, wait just a minute,
Isn't it grand?
Nothing is missing;
It's in my left hand!

I Swallowed My Gum

I feel so dumb; I swallowed my gum!
I wonder where it will go.
Will it keep going down as I jump all around?
Will it stop at the end of my toe?
The thought of it all just makes me quiver!
Oh, what am I going to do?

It could get stuck on my ribs or my liver,
Or maybe I'll get the flu.
Should I call a doctor or look for my mom,
Or maybe go find the police?
While I contemplate upon my fate,
I think I'll have another piece.

The Bubble

I blew a great big bubble
While chewing gum today.
It stretched out wide before it popped,
I'm really pleased to say.
A little gum got on my cheeks
And in my nose and hair.
My eyebrows felt a little weird,
But I didn't really care.

My ears were just a little plugged;
Some gum was on my chin.
The collar of my shirt
Was sticking to my skin.
The bubble was enormous;
The noise was very loud.
My mother wasn't happy,
But I was very proud!

Ink on My Finger

There's ink on my finger,
Oh, what should I do?
If I don't get it off,
All my skin will turn blue.

I'll be blue forever,
For twenty-one years.
I knew this would happen,
It was one of my fears.

I'd better do something
To help right away,
Or I will be blue
By the end of the day.

I could try some water,
Or maybe some soap.
If that doesn't work,
There will be no more hope.

I'd better act quickly,
I'd better not linger.
I must find a way
To get ink off my finger.

Register

Never put your head in a register,
For you just don't know what you'll find.
There could be some slugs or ten-legged bugs
Who might not be friendly or kind.

Never put your head in a register,
For you just don't know what you'll hear.
There might be a noise that could scare girls and boys,
So please, don't bring your head near.

What is behind those old registers?
What makes them whistle and blow?
What makes them howl?
What makes them creak?
No one will ever know.

So don't put your head in a register,
Children, you must beware!
If you ever see an old register,
Just pretend it isn't there.

Heebie Jeebies

Please don't scratch the chalkboard;
I just don't like that sound.
It gives me heebie jeebies,
And my skin crawls up and down.

When you eat your dinner,
Please don't scrape your plate.
I get the heebie jeebies
When I hear sounds I hate.

The heebie jeebies get me
When I see things I dread,
Like roaches in my closet
And spiders in my bed.

I get the heebie jeebies,
I shiver, shake, and squirm,
When deep inside my apple
I find a tiny worm.

Listen to me, children,
This warning is for you:
Be careful what you see and hear,
Or they may get you too!

The Walk

Every day at three o'clock
I walk my dog around the block.
He chases birds and bumblebees
And barks at butterflies and trees.

I feel the wind against my face,
Walking at our rapid pace.
I wave at neighbors passing by
But seldom stop for their reply.

I huff and puff and try to keep up,
Walking the block with my frisky pup.
We go so fast we almost *zoom*.
I'm just not sure who's walking whom.

Pets

I told my mom we needed a pet,
So I caught a friendly frog.
The friendly frog hopped away;
We bought a darling dog.

The darling dog barked all night—
We couldn't handle that!
We sold him to a hunter,
And we bought a quiet cat.

The quiet cat was soft and cute,
She purred a quiet purr.
She shredded all our curtains
And filled our house with fur.

We gave her to a farmer
Who offered us a horse,
But living in the city,
That wouldn't work, of course.

We bought some frisky goldfish
At the fish and turtle store.
Since I forgot to feed them,
They're not frisky anymore.

We took a pair of hamsters
When our neighbors moved away,
But soon we counted twenty-six;
The hamsters could not stay.

We tried a lot of different pets
Till Mother had enough.
The only pets that we have now
Are furry, cute, and stuffed!

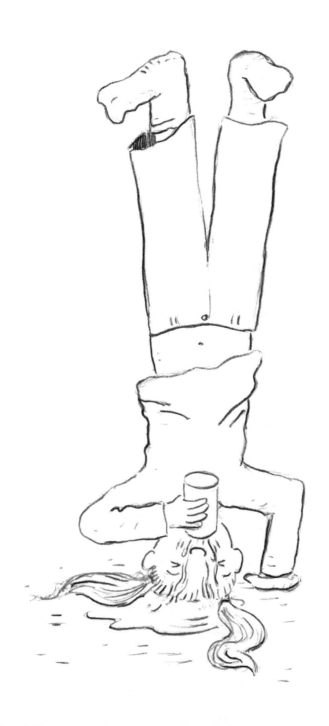

Hiccups

I had a case of hiccups
Just the other day.
I tried most every remedy
To make them go away.

I drank a glass of water,
I drank some soda pop.
I held my breath till I was blue,
But still, they did not stop.

I turned around in circles,
And on my head I stood.
I even tried to scare myself,
But still, it did no good.

I couldn't stop my hiccups
So I went outside to play.
When I forgot I had them,
My hiccups went away.

Fishin' and Kissin'

If I go fishin'
I might catch a fish,
Sit on the dock,
And make a fine wish.
Dangle my toes in the rippling brook,
Play with the minnows that nibble my hook.

But if I go kissin'
I might catch a cold.
I might get pneumonia,
Or so I've been told.
I might get a crush or a sad broken heart.
I might end up crying, so why should I start?

I've thought and I've thought
About all I'd be missin'—
I'm not going kissin'
I'd rather go fishin'!

Tommy

Tommy ate my goldfish;
I can't believe it's true!
Three were swimming yesterday
And now there's only two.

Tommy's always naughty,
My mother's really mad.
Tommy's going to get it,
And he's going to get it bad!

My mother scolded Tommy
And sent him to his bed.
"Tommy gets no supper!"
My mother firmly said.

I know that Tommy's sorry,
But he can't tell her that.
He's not a boy or grown-up,
He's just a naughty cat!

I Wish I Were an Octopus

I wish I were an octopus
With extra arms and legs.
I'd bake a batch of cookies
While I cooked some scrambled eggs.

I'd pet my furry kitten,
Sew a button on my sweater,
While I did my math assignment
And I wrote my friend a letter.

I'd make my bed and tie my shoes,
I'd brush my teeth and hair,
I'd straighten out my dresser drawers
While folding underwear.

I'd play a game of checkers,
Drink some cocoa from a mug,
But still I'd have an extra arm
To give my mom a hug.

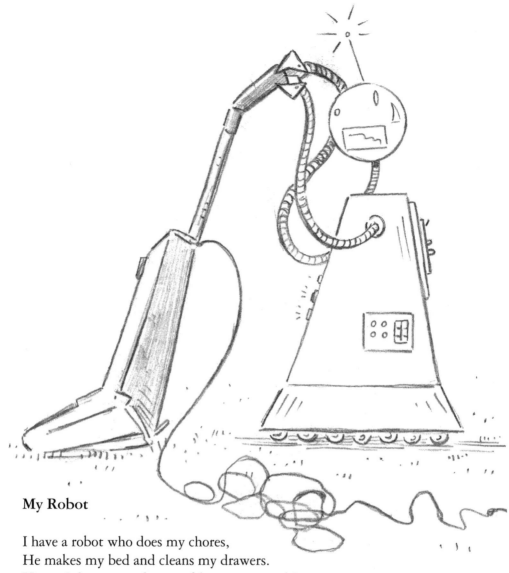

My Robot

I have a robot who does my chores,
He makes my bed and cleans my drawers.
He straightens my closet and hangs up my shirt,
He dusts the shelves to get rid of the dirt.

He vacuums the rug and washes the dishes,
He walks the dog and feeds the fishes.
He does my homework, my spelling and math.
I only wish he could take my bath.

Silly Things

Some things seem rather silly to me:
Potatoes have eyes,
But they cannot see.

A table has legs, but it doesn't walk.
A river has a mouth,
But I've never heard one talk.

A head of lettuce doesn't have hair.
You'll never get a hug
From the arms of a chair.

A saw has teeth, but it doesn't chew.
An ear of corn
Will not listen to you.

A shoe has a tongue, but it doesn't lick.
A ruler has a foot,
But I've never seen one kick.

Oranges have navels, and celery has hearts.
I think it's rather silly
When things have body parts!

Which Side?

One day when I was grumpy,
My mother smiled and said,
"You got up this morning,
On the wrong side of your bed."

Ever since that day,
I've tried to figure out,
Which side I should get in,
And which side I should get out.

So sometimes when I'm grumpy,
And it's not a pleasant day,
I jump back into bed
And get out a different way.

Beneath My Bed

I do not like to go to bed
And lie there for awhile,
Because I know a crocodile,
Who has a large suspicious smile,
Lives underneath my bed.
I almost want to scream and shout
When Father turns the hall light out,
Because I know the snakes come out
From underneath my bed.

I don't dare move, I lie so still,
Because I know the monsters will
Sit upon my windowsill.
They're underneath my bed.
I fall asleep though anyway
And wake up with the light of day.
The creatures all have gone away,
Back beneath my bed.

My Room

I hate to clean my bedroom,
But my mother says I must.
She doesn't like the messy floor,
The fingerprints, or dust.

I think it's quite attractive
With an interesting decor.
I've piled all my dirty clothes
So neatly on the floor.

My soccer ball and baseball
Are much easier to find,
Sitting on my windowsill
Beneath my mini blind.

The candy wrappers on my desk
Are really not that old.
The pop cans on my bookshelf
Look great with all that mold.

The cobwebs do not bother me;
In fact, I think they're nice.
The cookie crumbs beneath my bed
Have helped to feed the mice.

I like collecting magazines;
I need one hundred more.
It only takes a day or two
To close my closet door.

I'm very safe and comfortable
Within my private room.
I think I'll stay for twenty years
And never use a broom.

Bedtime

One thing that I really dread
Is when I have to go to bed,
Especially when I'm wide awake—
It makes no sense for goodness' sake!
Then after counting ninety sheep,
I close my eyes and fall asleep.

Then Mother comes to wake me up.
(She sometimes has to shake me up!)
But I would rather stay in bed—
It makes no sense, just like I said.
I think that I should sleep all day,
'Cause nighttime is the time to play.

Don't Forget to Say Your Prayers!

Dear God I know you're by my side
No matter where I go.
And I should never be afraid,
My mama told me so.

But when it's time to go to bed,
And I turn out the light,
It makes me very glad to know
That you stay up all night!

Thunderstorm

Pitter, patter goes the rain
On my bedroom windowpane.
Lightning flashing bold and bright,
Thunder crashing in the night.
Outside looms a thunderstorm;
Inside I am safe and warm.
Soon the storm will go away;
In my room is where I'll stay.

    CRASH!
    FLASH!
    BANG!
    BOOM!

Hey, Mom! I'm sleeping in your room!

Crystal Bowman loves writing for children and is the author of many books, including *If Peas Could Taste Like Candy, Ivan and the Dynamos,* and *Mommy May I Hug the Fishes?* Besides writing books, she enjoys inspiring students by sharing her poems and stories during elementary and middle school visits. A former schoolteacher and the mother of three grown children, Crystal currently lives with her husband in Michigan.